Y0-BEB-883

TIM.

IT IS SO GREAT TO FINALLY MEET YOU. YOUR PASSION IS TRULY CONTAGIOUS & INSPIRATIONAL

ALL THE BEST.

Saint Louis

SEEN *and* UNSEEN

Michael Kilfoy

A St. Louis Illustrated Book

St. Louis Seen and Unseen

Virginia Publishing Company
P.O. Box 4538
St. Louis Missouri 63108
314-367-6612
www.stl-books.com

Written, photoedited and designed by
Michael Kilfoy
Studio X, St. Louis, Missouri
314-773-8900
www.studiox.us

Photoeditorial assistance by
Ryan Asher and Amanda Wilson

Historical editorial assistance by
Ron Elz, AKA Johnny Rabbitt

Edited by Fran Levy and Jeff Fister

ISBN: 1-891442-38-4

Library of Congress Control Number:
2005938963

Printed in China

alzheimer's association

A major part of the profits of this book will go to the Alzheimer's Association, St. Louis Chapter. Special thanks to Sandy Jaffe for his support and advice.

Many of the images in this book will be offered as high-quality digital prints online at www.stlouisillustrated.com.

VIRGINIA PUBLISHING

Photographers:

Scott R. Avetta
Greg Barth
Michael Bizelli
Doug Caldwell
Michael DeFilippo
Alex Duenwald
Sam Fentress
Shellee Graham
Chris Hammond
Molly Hayden
Joseph Holst
David Kennedy
Michael Kilfoy
Ken Konchel
Hank Krishman
Greg Lappin
Jane Linders
Ray Marklin
James McKenzie
Jon Miller
John Nagel
Alise O'Brien
Victor Panchot
Lew Portnoy
Scott Raffe
Bob Reuter
Thomas Rollins
Steve Schulte
Wm. Stage
Steve Stelzer
David Stradal
David Torrence
Barbara Zucker

Greg Lappin

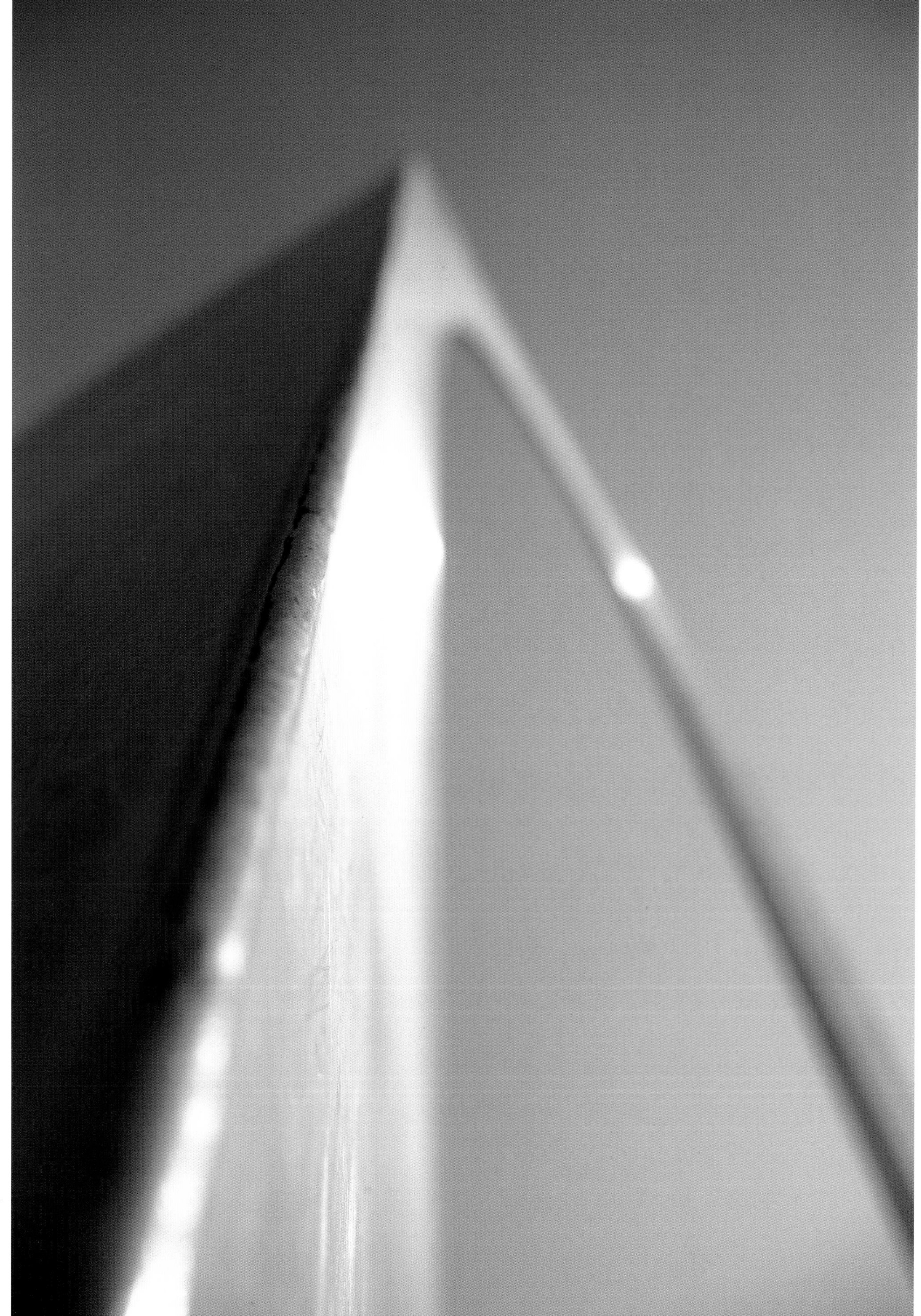

Joseph Holst

Preface

When I moved to St. Louis in 1983, I really didn't know what to make of it. It had a declining population and looked more to me like a city recently abandoned by a bunch of weary industrialists than a cool place to live. Within a few months that view quickly changed. It seemed as though much of St. Louis was tucked away in out-of-the-way corners, each having its own flavor and story. My line to out-of-town friends — and some in-town — was that St. Louis was a great place to live, but I wouldn't want to visit.

St. Louis has had plenty of time to become what it is. It is older than many cities to its east and practically everything to its west. It has been vastly different things at different points in time. More than any other place I have lived, St. Louis' history is a platform from which we create our future. Visually, you can't help but see the layers of its history present in so many places.

Doing what I do, I see the world in a different light. I favor the road less traveled, and, more to the point, the view less seen. When we are children, everything we see is new. We stare in awe at the world around us. As adults, we take much of what we see for granted. We don't often get to see something we know through a new set of eyes, and when we do, it is a wonderful thing. And, I hope, many of the following images will allow us to do just that.

The book you are holding in your hands is a brief, visual essay of an amazing place. Some of the people and places shown are well known, some are not. The images in this book are by dozens of photographers who call, or have called, St. Louis their home. Through their lenses, you may be able to see our city with new eyes.

Michael Kilfoy *January, 2006*

Lew Portnoy

It all begins with the river. St. Louis' reason for being is its location on the mighty Mississippi. These riverboats remind us of its past and its relationship to the great waterway.

Doug Caldwell

Thomas Rollins

Mike DeFilippo

A summer carriage ride
along the riverfront.
A little arch of water
is a playful expression
of the one behind the
photographer.

Alex Duenwald

Joseph Holst

Lew Portnoy

Not surprisingly, we received more photos of the Arch than any other single landmark. It is the most universal symbol of our city.

Doug Caldwell

Steve Stelzer

Lew Portnoy

Downtown at dusk during a Cardinals baseball game. Union Station and the Carl Milles Meeting of the Waters *fountain that graces it across Market Street.*

Many faces of the City Museum: The sculpted walls of the Enchanted Caves. A welder works on a platform on the MonstroCity. A museum-hosted boxing match.

Hank Krishman

Michael Bizelli

Bob Reuter

With dangerous abandon, a member of Pandora's Matchbox performs before a crowd at the Schlafly Brewery and Tap Room in midtown. They are headquartered at the City Museum.

Mike DeFilippo

Hank Krishman

Walter Hancock's statue of COURAGE *stands guard outside the World War I memorial. Our City Hall is designed after the city hall of Paris and is currently presided over by Mayor Francis G. Slay (center bottom right).*

Victor Panchot

David Torrence

Greg Lappin

Michael Bizelli

The rotunda of the Old Court House. Downtown lit up during Fair St. Louis. The balcony atop Washington University's Pediatric Research Building, overlooking downtown.

Ray Marklin

Sam Fentress

Greg Barth

Michael Bizelli

It almost appears as though the two Busch Stadiums form a single coliseum with breaks where they connect. The new Busch Stadium will be the third one in the Redbirds' history to bear that name.

PUJOLS

Michael Kilfoy

A Cardinals game during the team's final season at Busch Stadium. The view just seemed to be much too big to capture with only one photograph.

Joseph Holst

The entry to the Hyatt at Union Station as seen through the snow. Through those doors and up some stairs you will find the Great Hall. Union Station was at the center of the nation's busy train traffic before it eventually closed. ESCAPE FROM NEW YORK *was filmed here before Union Station was renovated in 1985.*

Joseph Holst

Michael Bizelli

Lew Portnoy

Doug Caldwell

This stone eagle, which looks not unlike the Maltese Falcon, sits perched in front of the Anheuser-Busch Brewery. The flying neon eagle on Highway 40 once flew at the old Sportsman's Park baseball stadium.

Michael Bizelli

In January 1999, Pope John Paul II makes the first-ever papal visit to St. Louis. More than 100,000 people crowd the TWA Dome as the determined pontiff celebrates mass. According to America's Center, this was not only the largest indoor crowd ever assembled in St. Louis, but in the entire United States.

The Clark Bridge (upper left), the Jefferson Barracks Bridge (lower left), and the Eads Bridge connect St. Louis to its neighbors in Illinois.

Jane Linders

Ken Konchel

Doug Caldwell

Washington University's Brookings Hall served as the headquarters for the city's 1904 World's Fair. Gargoyles adorn its gothic architecture.

All: Greg Lappin

Greg Lappin

Views of the St. Louis Cathedral Basilica. The walls and ceilings of the church are covered with the world's largest mosaic collection, with 41.5 million pieces of colored glass depicting religious scenes.

Greg Lappin

Greg Barth

Greg Lappin

The castle-like Eden Seminary in Webster Groves, blanketed in snow. Welcoming someone with open arms to the hereafter, this statue of Jesus stands at Laurel Hills Memorial Gardens in north St. Louis County.

Jane Linders

Jane Linders

The historic and side-by-side Calvary and Bellefontaine cemeteries in north St. Louis contain the graves of some of the city's best-known families, from explorer William Clark to playwright Tennessee Williams. The cemeteries were established far from the city's downtown because of a cholera outbreak in the mid-1800s.

Jane Linders

David Torrence

An opulent hall in the Masonic Temple and, at right, its exterior. The interior of the temple is a series of enormous meeting rooms and halls. When it was built in 1924, it was the most expensive building ever constructed in St. Louis.

Michael Kilfoy

St. Francis Xavier College Church, on the campus of St. Louis University in midtown, features the longest center aisle in the city. The Moolah Temple has been recently renovated by Amrit and Amy Gill.

Scott R. Avetta

Michael Kilfoy

A youth orchestra performs in Forest Park. These teens catch a limousine downtown after prom. At right, the new Cor Jesu High School, designed by alumna Carol Rusche Bentel, FAIA.

Lew Portnoy

Mike DeFilippo

Sam Fentress

Sam Fentress

Greg Barth

University City Hall was built in 1803 to be the headquarters of E.G. Lewis' publishing company. The octagonal building is capped by a copper dome and searchlight. Lewis was an urban visionary and feminist who published women's magazines.

The University City 'Loop' was named for the trolley cars that once ran down Delmar Boulevard. Here, diners enjoy themselves across from the Pageant. Pin-Up Bowl is frequented by rapper and U-City native Nelly. The historic Tivoli Theatre was renovated in 1995.

Jon Miller

James McKenzie

Alise O'Brien

All: Michael Kilfoy

A little girl twirls a sparkler at Bill Kwapy's 30th annual 4th of July party at Lake Teekawitha, just outside of St. Louis County. The annual Webster Groves parade is always a crowd pleaser.

David Torrence

A Ferris Wheel at the Thurtene Festival at Washington University. The entrance sign at the Skyview in Belleville is a reminder of the heyday of drive-in theaters.

David Torrence

David Torrence

Lew Portnoy

Chris Hammond

Life in the fast lane: the Pinewood Derby at the Italian "Hill" section of the city; Fairmont Park horse racing in Illinois; and the Lafayette Park Bike Race.

Bob Reuter

A dog gets in on the action at a Hoosierweight boxing match in a backyard in south city. Sadly, in St. Louis, a hoosier is not someone from Indiana. A cowgirl acts as a ringgirl to announce the round.

Bob Reuter

James McKenzie

The only thing more eclectic than the music may be the art on the walls at Joe's Café. Toledo sings twenty kinds of cool at the Delmar Lounge.

Bob Reuter

Two wizards and their fire-breathing retriever cast a spell on onlookers at the annual Soulard Mardi Gras parade. A carousel at the reopening of the Eads bridge.

Michael Bizelli

Mike DeFilippo

Michael Kilfoy

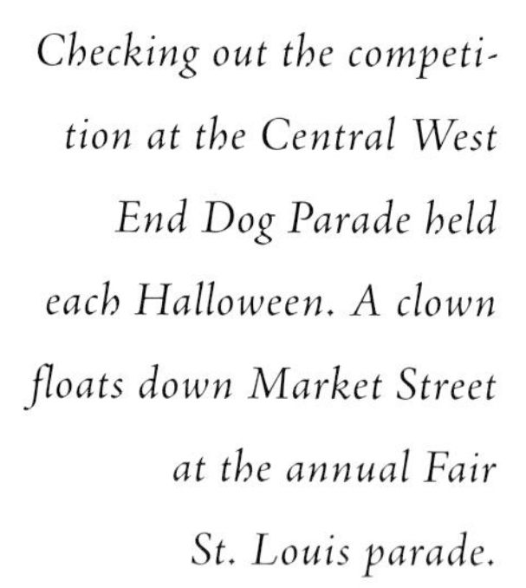

Checking out the competition at the Central West End Dog Parade held each Halloween. A clown floats down Market Street at the annual Fair St. Louis parade.

Michael Kilfoy

Lew Portnoy

Scott Raffe

Circus Flora was named after an orphaned, baby African elephant that founder David Balding rescued from Africa. Flora performed with the one-ring circus until her retirement in 2000. The circus has a small, intimate atmosphere.

Bob Reuter

Wm. Stage

The Amish people pictured just add to the cross-section of people at the Greyhound bus depot. These veterans join the annual Veterans' Day Parade on motorcycle.

Wm. Stage

Mike DeFilippo

A saxophonist jams at the St. Louis Jazz Festival. Texas Rockabilly singer Kim Lenz performs at the Hi-Pointe Lounge at the city's western edge.

Bob Reuter

The St. Louis Perfectos baseball club plays ball by circa 1868 rules. Here they play at Lafayette Park against the Unions of West Florissant.

David Torrence

David Torrence

LIVE QUIETLY
CITY ORDINANCES PRO-
HIBIT CONSUMPTION OF
ALCOHOLIC BEVERAGES
ON ANY STREET, SIDE-
WALK, PARKING LOT OR
ALLEY IN THE CITY. VIOLA-
TIONS OF THIS ORDINANCE
ARE PUNISHABLE BY A FINE
IMPRISONMENT FOR NOT
MORE THAN NINETY DAYS.
PA
SHAME CLUB
EIFFEL
Marshall

Michael Kilfoy

The almost-famous Microwave Society rocks the Hi-Pointe at an all-teen event.

Molly Hayden

Ray Marklin

St. Louis' version of Burning Man: the Arteca tower burns along the riverfront. Big River Hurricane Katrina Relief Benefit at the historic Sheldon Concert Hall, one of the world's most acoustically perfect music venues.

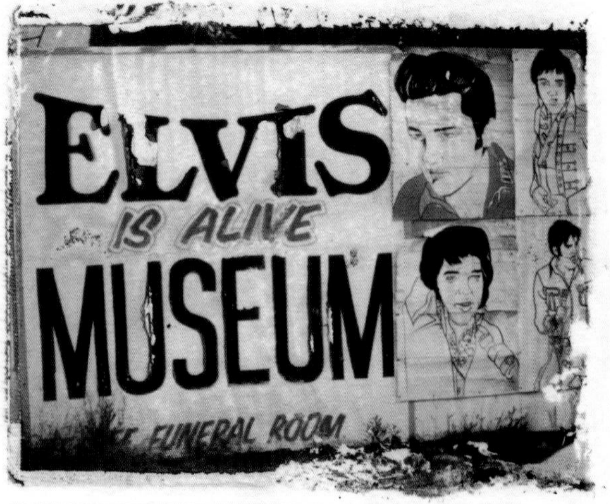

Jane Linders

Mike DeFilippo

At left, the Elvis Museum pays homage to the King. Outside of the main Post Office, Elvis impersonator #9 pays a little homage as well.

All: Scott Raffe

The Cardinals aren't the only game in town. The minor league River City Rascals in St. Charles keep the small-town baseball spirit alive.

Bob Reuter

Mike DeFilippo

Sullen, left, performs at The Way Out Club in south city. Ozomatli has the crowd calling out for more at downtown's Taste of St. Louis.

Little Killers perform at Frederick's Music Lounge. At right, these urban cowboys set about to bustin' a 55-gallon bronco, south city style, at the Southside Backyard BBQ and Rodeo.

Bob Reuter

Bob Reuter

Steve Schulte

Steve Schulte

Life in the fast lane: stunt pilots at the St. Louis County Fair and Air Show at Spirit of St. Louis Airport. A tattoo artist makes a lasting impression during the Tattoo Expo at the City Museum.

Mike DeFilippo

David Stradal

With a little luck, the Americans will once again defeat the Germans, and the North will beat the South, in reenacted battles at Jefferson Barracks.

Lew Portnoy

David Torrence

Landmarks Association, a local preservation group, is trying to save the 1863 Clemens house on Cass Avenue in north St. Louis. It was once the home of Mark Twain's cousin, James Clemens, Jr.

David Torrence

The Lemp mansion housed the family of St. Louis' biggest brewery before Prohibition in 1919 forced its closure. The Lemps were also one of the city's most tragic families; three Lemp suicides occurred in the house, and many believe it is haunted.

All: David Torrence

The Eugene Field House and Toy Museum was Eugene's childhood home. Many of the toys in this room were used by the popular poet.

65.
50
68.
29.

John Nagel

David Torrence

Left, Greystone, a Gothic Revival house in Pevely, south of St. Louis. Monk's Mound at Cahokia Mounds State Historic Site, just east of the city. The mounds are all that remain of the Mississippian Indians. Monks Mound is considered the largest prehistoric earthen mound in the New World.

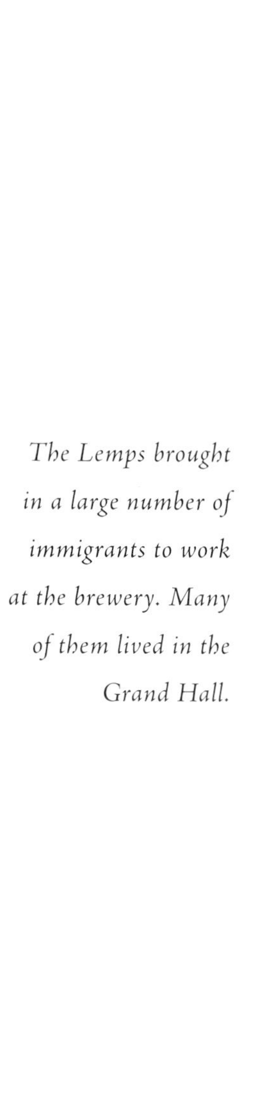

The Lemps brought in a large number of immigrants to work at the brewery. Many of them lived in the Grand Hall.

David Torrence

John Nagel

Holy Corners historic district in the Central West End features a number of historic churches near the corner of Kingshighway and Washington boulevards. This is a detail from St. John's Methodist Church, built in 1901.

James McKenzie

Greg Rhomberg's Antique Warehouse has amassed what is considered the largest private collection of Americana in St. Louis. His trove spans the period of time from the Industrial Revolution through the 1970s.

Greg Lappin

The power of prayer. Many people call, email or write to the Holy Spirit Adoration Sisters, also known as the Pink Sisters, to pray for them. It is believed that they have a more direct line to the divine.

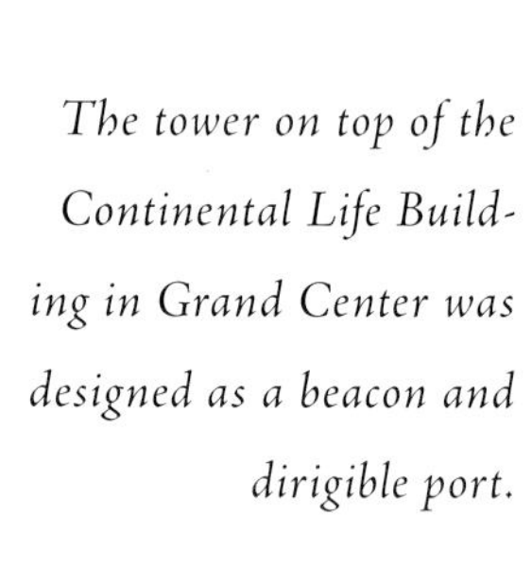

The tower on top of the Continental Life Building in Grand Center was designed as a beacon and dirigible port.

Doug Caldwell

Greg Lappin

Jane Linders

'Eat rite or don't eat at all!' proclaims the Eat-Rite Diner. Italian bakery Amighetti's is a long-time favorite on the Hill.

David Torrence

Americana signage in the heartland: Saleem's in University City, Fast Eddie's in Alton, Ted Drewes and Phil's BBQ.

Scott R. Avetta

Scott R. Avetta

David Torrence

Scott R. Avetta

Shellee Graham

Good taste in St. Louis: Spencer's Grill in Kirkwood and Federhofer's in Affton are long-standing favorites in St. Louis.

Scott R. Avetta

Shellee Graham

The Chain of Rocks bridge once carried weary travelers on Route 66 from Illinois to St. Louis. It is now a popular pedestrian bridge with unmatched views of downtown St. Louis, and of bald eagles in winter. Often mentioned, rarely eaten, brains don't come any cheaper.

Wm. Stage

Lg Yellow
Red
ONION
$1.25 lb

All: David Torrence

Established in 1836, the Soulard Farmer's Market is one of the oldest public markets still in existence in the United States. I've often thought of it as one of the most cosmopolitan places in St. Louis, where people from all walks of life shop alongside one another.

Views of the lily ponds and Carl Milles' 1949 ANGEL MUSICIANS *near the east entrance, as seen at right, which was once the original entrance, of the Missouri Botanical Garden.*

All: Greg Lappin

Steve Stelzer

Jane Linders

Lew Portnoy

The Climatron at the Missouri Botanical Garden was designed by East St. Louis' R. Buckminster Fuller. Seven Bridges in the Japanese Gardens. Some koi swim beneath.

Scott R. Avetta

Catch me if you can. Henry Shaw designed a maze for Tower Grove Park. Many years later, this one was created behind his country residence. A Victorian reflecting ball mirrors everything but the photographer in the eastern garden of the house.

Scott R. Avetta

Michael Kilfoy

Greg Lappin

A pair of weeping lions at the main entrance of Tower Grove Park are copies of those on the tomb of Pope Clement XIII. Shown at dusk, the Milles sculpture garden features seven bronze statues by Swedish culptor Carl Milles.

Michael Kilfoy

The Sons of Rest Pavilion, built in 1872 in Tower Grove Park, is a perfect picnic spot. The park director's home was once a model home for a series of villas conceived by Henry Shaw that were to line the parkside of Magnolia and Arsenal Avenues.

Michael Kilfoy

Scott R. Avetta

Michael Kilfoy

Michael Kilfoy

Dead poet's society: Tower Grove Park has statues of a number of pre-twentieth century luminaries, including these of poet Friedrich von Schiller, German botanist Alexander Von Humbolt and William Shakespeare.

Greg Lappin

Mike DeFilippo

Behind the Magic House in Kirkwood you will find a statue of children dancing in a circle, also known as The Circle of Peace *by Gary Price. The young ladies of Mary Institute, a private school, dance annually around the Maypole. This tradition dates back centuries.*

David Torrence

David Torrence

The Compton Heights Water Tower, which stands 179 feet tall, was built to allow consistent water pressure throughout its surrounding area. Here is a rustic view of the exterior and a view of downtown as seen from the tower.

Fire and Ice exhibit at Laumeier Sculpture Park. Alexander Liberman's The Way, as seen at dusk, is their signature sculpture.

Ray Marklin

Ray Marklin

The Fabulous Fox was opened in 1929 at a time when the imagination of movie theater architects was not to be outdone by the films the theaters showed. It was lovingly restored by Leon and Mary Strauss in 1982. Here is an interior detail and its grand stage.

Michael Kilfoy

Sam Fentress

David Torrence

We recently learned that this French Village sign in East St. Louis was taken down and bought by the Antique Warehouse (page 98) for its collection. The Wildley in Edwardsville, Illinois, and another view of the Fabulous Fox.

Greg Lappin

Lew Portnoy

The Daniel Boone house was home to the famous pioneer in his latter years, until his death in 1820. The Georgian-style home was built beginning in 1803 by Nathan Boone, Daniel's son. A lone deer stands on a ridge at Lone Elk Park.

All: Scott R. Avetta

This lake and boathouse at Carondelet Park was built in 1875. The park was spearheaded by Hiram Leffingwell, who also was responsible for developing Forest Park and O'Fallon Park.

Grant's Farm is the south St. Louis County home of the Busch brewery family and is open for tours. Here, people stroll through a Germanic gate, and young Clydesdales kick up their heels at the farm.

Scott R. Avetta

Lew Portnoy

Lew Portnoy

The St. Louis Zoo is recognized as one of the country's finest. The World's Fair Pavilion is just one part of a recent $100 million renovation of Forest Park.

Alise O'Brien

More Forest Park scenes: The Science Center from the south side of Highway 40. The Municipal Opera of St. Louis, also known as The Muny. The Jefferson Memorial Building, which houses the History Museum and the Missouri Historical Society, was built from funds from the World's Fair.

Lew Portnoy

Lew Portnoy

David Kennedy

Joseph Holst

Each year, the night before the Great Forest Park Balloon Race, entrants light up Forest Park with their balloons in what is called the Balloon Glow.

Barbara Zucker

The race attracts more than 70 balloonists from around the country and more than 100,000 spectators, making it the state's largest single-day sporting event and fund-raiser for Forest Park. Pilots donate their time and compete for prizes such as a broken toaster. Some balloons end up in city streets; others have landed in the river. Mostly, the balloonists just have fun. "Soft landings" is their battle cry.

Joseph Holst

Greg Barth

Barbara Zucker

The Floral Conservatory of St. Louis, also known as the Jewel Box, as viewed from the exterior and interior.

Ken Konchel

Lew Portnoy

Something old and something new. The Pulitzer Foundation for the Arts in Grand Center (left) and The St. Louis Art Museum in Forest Park.

The eternal symbol of the city: a statue of St. Louis ix looks over Forest Park's Grand Basin. A child waits by the water for the Great Forest Park Balloon Race.

Greg Lappin

Michael Bizelli

Greg Lappin

The sculpture of P*AINTING* *graces the front of the St. Louis Art Museum. The Nathan Frank bandstand in front of the Muny. A boy rests on a turtle at Turtle Park. The turtles were created by City Museum's Bob Cassilly.*

Scott R. Avetta

Lew Portnoy

The Grand Basin at the foot of Art Hill, which once was capped by the Festival Hall at the 1904 World's Fair. A series of cascades flowed into it. Here the Grand Basin is shown at twilight.

All: Greg Lappin

Michael Kilfoy

The Photographers

Scott R. Avetta
314-487-3280
Scott documents the natural beauty of the midwest and Ozark region. His work has been published extensively. He also teaches photography at the Missouri Botanical Garden.

Greg Barth
www.gregbarth.com
314-283-8871
Greg shoots beautiful, large-format photography for fine art and commercial venues. His work is often seen at local galleries and art shows.

Michael Bizelli
www.bizelliphotography.com
314-890-9084
Growing up working in his father's portrait studio in St. Charles, Michael found his passion for photography, and has never looked back. He has worked professionally as a corporate/commercial photographer for more than thirty years.

Doug Caldwell
314-984-8229
Specializing in fine art landscapes and cityscapes, Doug has made photography his passion since 1990.

Michael DeFilippo
www.michaeldefilippo.com
314-421-5817
Michael once said, "I'm the guy you hire to shoot the Battle of Armageddon. I get the shot before most photographers unpack their gear."

Alex Duenwald
alejandroisonline.com
314-481-8510
Alex is a graphic designer with a strong interest in architectural photography. Through his camera, he documents the beauty of the architecture and detail that St. Louis offers in abundance.

Sam Fentress
314-721-4187
www.samfentress.com
Sam has photographed architecture and interiors for more than 20 years. He has been extensively published worldwide, and his images appear in the collections of several major museums.

Shellee Graham
314-298-3839
Ms. Route 66. Shellee was awarded the John Steinbeck Award from the National Historic Route 66 Federation, and is the author of a book on the Coral Courts. She has extensively documented life along the famous thoroughfare.

Chris Hammond
www.chrishammond.com
636-527-1765
Chris is an avid weekend race car driver, and his love for photography is an outgrowth of his love for racing and all things fast.

Molly Hayden
www.studio7network.com
314-398-5532
Molly is a versatile photographer, best known for her exquisite fashion and studio work.

Joseph Holst
www.jyoseph.com
314-369-1281
Joseph's love for St. Louis is evident in his grassroots approach to photography on his personal photoblog site. He is also the creator of a blog for local photographers at www.stlphotoblogs.com.

David Kennedy
www.showmephotos.com
314-771-4826
David has worked for years as a photojournalist. He loves telling a good story, especially with his camera.

Michael Kilfoy
www.studiox.us
314-773-8900
Michael is a designer, illustrator, marketer, fine artist and photographer. Using the credo "a great photo is a beautiful lie," he loves to recreate reality when given the opportunity.

Ken Konchel
www.kenkonchelphoto.com
314-727-4116
Ken is drawn to the expressive power of buildings, and his passion is recording their forms in provocative ways. He exhibits extensively at galleries and art shows throughout the country.

Greg Lappin
www.greglappinphotography.com
314-394-1746
Greg has a unique vision that transcends any single genre. His primary focus is people, and his clients range from soon-to-be-married couples to major ad agencies throughout the country.

Hank Krishman
708-790-8375
www.hkdigitalphoto.com

Jane Linders
314-576-7155
www.janelinders.focalfix.com
Jane works primarily in Polaroid photo transfers, lifts and infrared photography. Her work appears regularly in area galleries and art shows.

Ray Marklin
www.raymarklin.com
314-772-2478
Ray's work of more than three decades spans across the globe, documenting life wherever he goes. He has been published extensively, and his work appears in many major corporate collections.

James McKenzie
www.massiveimageworks.com
314-703-5716
James is a new photo talent to St. Louis. Although he is a very versatile shooter, his background is primarily journalistic, and he is exceptional at capturing the moment.

Jon Miller
312-321-1151
www.hedrichblessing.com

John Nagel
www.jwnagel.com
573-486-1139
John is the director of The Center for Visual Technology at St. Louis Community College at Meramec. His work appears in several major corporate collections and museums.

Alise O'Brien
314-721-0285
www.aliseobrienphotography.com
Open any interior design magazine and chances are you'll find a photograph by Alise. She is considered one of the top architectural and interior photographers in the country.

Victor P. Panchot
314-776-2180
www.bluemonkeyltd.com
Victor describes himself as an artist, carpenter, furniture maker, free thinker, risk taker and occasional photographer.

Lew Portnoy
www.lewportnoy.com
314-432-2828
Lew is the godfather of location photography in St. Louis. He and long-time partner Lois Constantz have an immense catalog of work that spans more than three decades.

Scott Raffe
www.raffephoto.com
918-494-5001
At one time, Scott called St. Louis home. Now his studio is in Tulsa. Most of his compelling work consists of photographing people, animals, or a combination of both.

Bob Reuter
www.mphase.com/reuter1.htm
Bob is our unofficial chronicler of nightlife in St. Louis. He is the host of BOB'S SCRATCHY RECORDS *on* KDHX-FM *as well as an accomplished musician, and shows his work regularly at local galleries.*

Tom Rollins
618-281-5385
Tom's passion for photography has taken him to every continent on the globe. He shoots commercially across the country and is currently the staff photographer for the World Bird Sanctuary.

Steve Schulte
www.steveschulte.com
314-313-1622
Steve loves aviation and photography, and any combination of the two.

Wm. Stage
www.pixofpeople.com
314-621-0412
A former photojournalism instructor at St. Louis University, Wm. Stage has photographed more than 8000 people since 1982. His work has appeared in numerous periodicals; his most recent book is PICTURES OF PEOPLE.

Steve Stelzer
www.aerialphotographs.com
314-313-1622/800-400-2627
First experimenting with aerial photography in 1991 using a mini-blimp, Steve has become one of the premier aerial photographers in the region.

David Stradal
www.stradal.com
314-821-6128
David shoots commercially as well as WWII *reenactments. Many of his shoots look like they are from the era of his nostalgic subject matter.*

Todd Thomas

Todd Thomas
314-588-9563
Todd is a wonderful photographer who experiments with photo processes, including Polaroid transfers, lifts, and various digital media.

David Torrence
www.davidtorrence.com
314-210-5406
David shoots commercially, with an emphasis on advertising and editorial work. He also shoots fine art photography, sometimes using vintage cameras. David loves the diverse architecture, history and old soul that St. Louis offers.

Barbara Zucker
www.bfzucker@aol.com
314-727-2683
Barbara works primarily in Polaroid photo transfers and lifts, and alternative processes. She has a large catalog of work and has been extensively published.

We would like to thank the following for their submissions:

Photographs of the City Museum by Hank Krishman, submitted by the City Museum.

Photograph of the Tivoli submitted by Joe Edwards.

Photograph of the Pageant submitted by Kiku Obata and Company.

Many of the images in this book have been scanned by Allied Photocolor, St. Louis, Missouri. 314-652-4000.

Joseph Holst

I am extremely grateful to all of my fellow photographers for their time and energy in putting together their work for this project. I have seen some incredible images. We could easily fill another book with all of the compelling photographs that we received. Maybe we will.

I would like to extend a very special thanks to the incomparable Ron Elz, AKA Johnny Rabbitt, who has spent countless hours relaying the histories of many of the places shown in this collection and quite a few that weren't. There are few images in this book about which he could not tell me at least a little something beyond what we already know. Some of these stories we really must get into another book.

Thanks also go to my friends and partners on this project, Jeff Fister and Sandy Jaffe, for having the faith in our vision and the confidence in us to see it through.